HOWARD DEVOTO

IT ONLY LOOKS AS IF IT HURTS

THE COMPLETE LYRICS 1976-1990

BLACK SPRING PRESS

It Only Looks As If It Hurts
first published by
BLACK SPRING PRESS Ltd.
46 Rodwell Road
London SE22

British Library Cataloguing in Publication Data
Devoto, Howard
It only looks as if it hurts : complete lyrics 1976-90.
I. Title
ISBN 0-948238-08-9

Designed by Damian Wayling
Photo-typeset by Repro-type London
Printed by WBC Print Ltd, Bristol

CONTENTS

1976-77

YOU TEAR ME UP

BREAKDOWN

FRIENDS OF MINE

ORGASM ADDICT

BOREDOM

TIME'S UP

LESTER SANDS
DROP IN THE OCEAN

LOVE BATTERY

BIG DUMMY

DON'T MESS ME ROUND

PEKING HOOLIGAN

YOU TEAR ME UP

Well I know it's the night
but have you gotta beat the daylights out of me
I'm getting so god-damned bruised
I'll soon be softer than a stoned cherry

And when you let your flesh creep over me
you know I don't know what's come over me
something about the way you drool and kiss
makes love seem nothing like this

You tear me up
you grab what's mine
you tear me up
every single time
you tear me up
what a hideous crime
you tear me up
you're a bloody swine

All this slurping and sucking
you know it's putting me off my food
you're noisier than a motorway
and about two times - three times as rude

You know you got such big eyes
they make me feel so small
my heart is only one mouthful
but you - you can have it all

You're just as hard as a pavement
and I don't know where my passion went
you think that maybe I could walk on you
you'd make a damned good anaesthetic - I'll say that for you

BREAKDOWN

If I seem a little jittery I can't restrain myself
I'm falling into fancy fragments, can't contain myself
I'm gonna breakdown, breakdown yes
I'm gonna breakdown, breakdown yes

Now I can stand austerity but it gets a little much
when there's all these livid things that you never get to touch
I'm gonna breakdown, breakdown yes
I'm gonna breakdown, breakdown yes

I feel me brain like porridge coming out of me ears
and I was anticipating reverie
I've taken leave of me senses, and I'm in arrears
my legs buckle over, I'm living on my knees
I'm gonna breakdown yes
I'm gonna breakdown yes
I'm gonna breakdown yes

Whatever makes me tick it takes away my concentration
sets my hands a-trembling, gives me frustration
I'm gonna breakdown, breakdown yes
I'm gonna breakdown, breakdown yes

So I hear that two is company for me it's plenty trouble
though my doublethoughts are clearer now that I am seeing double
I'm gonna breakdown, breakdown yes
I'm gonna breakdown, breakdown yes

Oh mum can I grow out of what's too big for me?
I'll give up that ghost before it gives up me
I wander loaded as a crowd, a nowherewolf of pain
Living next to nothing, my nevermind remains
I'm gonna breakdown yes
I'm gonna breakdown yes
I'm gonna breakdown yes

FRIENDS OF MINE

Rita spits out her laurel leaf
and grabs a piece of my pie
she's gonna lead me up the mountain path
as the crows fly

Claudette's pretty quick off the mark
like a polaris missile in heat
she smiles at a hundred miles an hour
and rushes you off your feet

There's all these friends of mine
they've got me suffering
they don't take a line
they keep me pissing adrenalin

Ratty is nearly unique
looks like a Pre-Raphaelite barb freak
wears dangerous jewellery
got a cast iron personality

Sandie wears an awful lot of silk
says she's a friend of Mr Acker Bilk
she's going out of my mind
wants to live on milk

There's all these friends of mine
they've got me suffering
they don't take a line
they keep me pissing adrenalin

I was musing on the pool outdoors
about foreign matters and fancy affairs
Betty trimmed my nails with pliers
while eating avocado pears

Norman's sobbing cos his make-up's
running away with itself
he's heading for an early grave
scared to death about the state of his health

There's all these friends of mine
they've got me suffering
they don't take a line
they keep me pissing adrenalin

ORGASM ADDICT

You tried it just for once
and found it alright for kicks
but now you've found out
it's a habit that sticks
you're an orgasm addict

Sneaking in the backdoor
with dirty magazines
your mother wants to know
what are those stains on your jeans
you're an orgasm addict

You get in heat
you get in a sulk
but you still keep beating
your meat to pulp
you're an orgasm addict

You're a kid casanova
you're no Joseph
it's a labour of love
fucking yourself to death
you're an orgasm addict

You're making out with schoolkids
winos and heads of state
you've even made it with the lady
who puts the little plastic robins
on the Christmas cakes
butchers' assistants and bellhops
you've had 'em all here and there
children of god
and the joystrings
international women with no body hair

So you're asking in an alley
and your voice ain't steady
the sex mechanic's rough
but you're more than ready
you're an orgasm addict

Johnny-want-fuckie
everywhere and all ways
he's got the energy
he will amaze
he's an orgasm addict
he's always at it
he's an orgasm addict

BOREDOM

Yeah, well, I say what I mean
I say what comes to my mind
I never get around to things
I live a straight, straight line

You know me - I'm acting dumb
you know the scene - very humdrum
boredom, boredom

I'm living in this movie
but it doesn't move me
I'm the man that's waiting for the phone to ring
Hear it ring-a-ding-a-fucking-ding

You know me - I'm acting dumb
you know the scene - very humdrum
boredom, boredom

You see there's nothing behind me
I'm already a has-been
my future ain't what it was
well I think I know the words that I mean

You know me - I'm acting dumb
you know the scene - very humdrum
boredom, boredom

B'dum, b'dum

I've taken this extravagant journey
so it seems to me
I just came from nowhere
and I'm going straight back there

You know me - I'm acting dumb
you know the scene - very humdrum
boredom, boredom

So I'm living in this movie
but it doesn't move me
so tell me who are you trying to arouse?
get your hands out of my trousers

You know me - I'm acting dumb
you know the scene - very humdrum
boredom, boredom

14 TIME'S UP

I bin waiting in the supermarket
standing in line with the beans (cash up)
I bin waiting at the post office
for sticky pictures of the queen (stick up)
now I'm waiting for you
to get yourself good 'n ready (make up)
thinking to myself is this what they mean
by going steady? (break up)
I bin waiting in the waiting room
and I've bin sitting in the sitting room
and now I'm whining in the dining room
"waiting for you's like waiting for the man in the moon"

I was really smouldering
seen the back of forty kingsize cigarettes (stood up)
this hanging on is murder
But if you'd just come along I'd have no regrets (give up)
and so I'd phone your number
and your mother tells me you're still in bed (get up)
when you come to the phone your voice is thick and sexy
goes straight to my head (shut up)
and I bin standing in the standing room
and I bin smoking in the smoking room
and now I'm dying in the living room
I'm gonna forget what I came for here real soon

Your time's up and me too
I'm out on account of you

I was really burned out and smouldering
seen the front and back of eighty kingsize cigarettes (stood up)
this hanging on is killing me
if you'd just creep along I'd have no regrets (give up)
and so I phone your grandmother
she says you're still in bed (get up)
when you get to the phone your voice is thick and sexy
shoots through the top of my head (shut up)
I bin standing in the standing room
I bin smoking in the smoking room
Now I'm dying in the living room
I'm gonna forget what I came for here real soon

Your time's up and me too
I'm out on account of you

LESTER SANDS
DROP IN THE OCEAN

Lester Sands has been working very hard
keeping up with what's gone down
Lester Sands is really in touch
with what is whose in town
Lester Sands bores the ass off me
Lester Sands is a bighead case
I am getting so sick of the sight
of Lester Sands' face

He thinks he'll be someone someday (no way)
he thinks he'll get somewhere someway (no way)
Lester Sands is a drop in the ocean
Lester Sands is a drop in the ocean
Lester Sands
drop in the ocean

He'd better pull himself together
do something speedy or else
Lester Sands will be shown the ropes
and Lester Sands will hang himself
Lester Sands bigmouth extraordinaire
he's pulled a muscle in his head
Lester Sands strings words together
cos his senses have fled

He thinks he'll be someone someday (no way)
he thinks he'll get somewhere someway (no way)
Lester Sands is a drop in the ocean
Lester Sands is a drop in the ocean
Lester Sands
drop in the ocean

Lester Sands is a stupid fucker
Lester Sands will stay that way
Lester Sands just gathers his trash
and brings it round every day
Lester Sands, think you'd better scram
if you wanna get out alive
or are you looking to get friendly
with somebody's bunches of fives

He thinks he'll be someone someday (no way)
he thinks he'll get somewhere someway (no way)
Lester Sands is a drop in the ocean
Lester Sands is a drop in the ocean
Lester Sands
drop in the ocean

LOVE BATTERY

My mad love battery - wants to charge you
my mad love battery - could maybe enlarge you
my mad love battery - fizzing at the terminals
my mad love battery - is one helluva pack of an animal

My mad love battery - has to have us both
my mad love battery - don't allow for sleep or sloth
my mad love battery - never minces words
don't discharge flattery, so don't listen to what you've heard

I got sick electricity
on the boil for you
I got this searing love
which burns without cue

My mad love battery - is running out of control
my mad love battery - is gonna swallow us whole
my mad love battery - never minces words
don't discharge flattery, so don't listen to what you've heard

I got this crazy current
gets into my underwear
and when it really connects
I come and go everywhere

My mad love battery - wants to charge you
my mad love battery - could maybe enlarge you
my mad love battery - fizzing at the terminals
my mad love battery - is one helluva pack of an animal

BIG DUMMY

You think I'm a lame duck
I don't give a blue fuck
I'm living like crazy
driven to be lazy

I blush like a tomato
pale as a chipped potato
you're a real peach
just out of reach

We're all cooking the same goose
a recipe of fiction
I stew in my own juice
in another kitchen

You think I'm a lame duck
I don't give a blue fuck
I don't give two hoots
you're too big for your bossy boots

DON'T MESS ME ROUND

Gonna have to cut you down to size
you're running out of style
I'm gonna kit you out
with a subterranean profile
don't you push me too far
it's gonna be bad for your health
you'll wind up just a friend
to the ghost of your former self

Don't mess me round
don't you mess me round
you put me down
don't mess me round

Any more of your mouth
and we'll both see red
I'll pin your bottom lip
to the top of your head
you've got too much talkie-talkie
don't say one more thing
I'll make your insides look
like a Jackson Pollock painting

Don't mess me round
don't you mess me round
you put me down
don't mess me round

PEKING HOOLIGAN

You know me cos I hang around the bicycle sheds
kicking over the traces in my fancy footwear
as I go wrecking and stealing
around Tiananmen Square

I'm a Peking hooligan
I'm a social problem
I'm a Peking hooligan

I just finished at the city schools
I don't want to go back to the fields
I paid no heed to Mao's words
I heard after every meal

I'm a Peking hooligan
I'm a social problem
I'm a Peking hooligan

1977-78

DEFINITIVE GAZE

I've got this bird's eye view
and it's in my brain
clarity has reared
its ugly head again
so this is real life
you're telling me
and everything
is where it ought to be

I like your nerve
I like watching you
but I don't watch what I'm doing
got better things to do
so this is real life
you're telling me
now I'm lost in shock
your face fits perfectly

MY TULPA

I suspect you ain't so sweet
as the lust I'm concealing
my skin will crawl back home to Ma
I've lost my way in my feelings

You always collect your fists
when my shadow falls upon your hands
you're just giving body heat away
but they say you're a nice enough young man

I want to see you
don't you want to see me?
I'm full of questions
you're full of mystery

You can touch yourself anytime
you can touch yourself anytime
I'm so wretched - you are so fetching
stop smiling at me - treat me unpleasantly

You've got the whole world in your wardrobe
your furniture's made to injure me
my skin will crawl back home to Ma
when our souls mingle uneasily

I want to see you
don't you want to see me?
I'm full of questions
you're full of mystery

SHOT BY BOTH SIDES

This and that, they must be the same
what is legal is just what's real
what I'm given to understand
is exactly what I steal
I wormed my way into the heart of the crowd
I wormed my way into the heart of the crowd
I was shocked to find what was allowed
I didn't lose myself in the crowd

Shot by both sides
on the run to the outside of everything
shot by both sides
they must have come to a secret understanding

New offences always in my nerves
they're taking my time by force
they all sound the same when they scream
as a matter of course
I wormed my way into the heart of the crowd
I wormed my way into the heart of the crowd
I was shocked to find what was allowed
I didn't lose myself in the crowd

Shot by both sides
on the run to the outside of everything
shot by both sides
they must have come to a secret understanding

'Why are you so edgy, kid?'
asks the man with the voice
one thing follows another
you live and learn, you have no choice
I wormed my way into the heart of the crowd
I wormed my way into the heart of the crowd
I was shocked to find what was allowed
I didn't lose myself in the crowd

I didn't lose myself in the crowd
but I worm my way

Shot by both sides
I don't ask who's doing the shooting
shot by both sides
we must have come to a secret understanding

RECOIL

Dashing through Paradise
so polite in what I say
lost in the age I'm in
I want a world to give away

I know what's mine
you'll learn what's yours
I know what you want to see
you scratch my back
and I grow claws
falling in love awkwardly

Dancing in my own good time
my words stick out of your face
if you're not feeling so weak today
somebody will take your place

I know what's mine
you'll learn what's yours
I know what you want to see
you scratch my back
and I grow claws
falling in love awkwardly

26 BURST

Once you had this promise
on the tip of your tongue
but it went without saying
it went on too long
all the straws you clutched at
have burst into flames
and so you smile that way
tantalisingly lame

The smart ones understand
how your heart bursts
like a bottle of champagne
your just desserts
the smart ones understand
you shouldn't settle for less
you're going to forget yourself
in my happiness

Keep your silence to yourself (in my happiness)
you will forget yourself (in my happiness)

MOTORCADE

I believe all that I read now
night has come off the corners
shadows flicker sweet and tame
dancing like crazy mourners
the man with the hotdogs sells lemonade
someone over there needs first aid
while me and the rest of the world
await the touch of the motorcade
no one finds time to turn a blind eye
you can't be too careful nowadays
and my friend says 'listen...
to the stupid things they're making you say'

Here comes the motorcade
moving so slow and hard
like a snake in a closet
holding sway in the boulevard
here is your man
all faces turn unanimously
the small fry who sizzle in his veins
in all security

In the back of his car
into the null and void he shoots
the man at the centre of the motorcade
has learned to tie his boots
in the back of his car
in the null and void he sees
the man at the centre of the motorcade
can choose between coffee and tea

In the boulevard - the motorcade holds sway

THE GREAT BEAUTICIAN IN THE SKY

Laughter staggers on
in between their gags
pounding their faces
he's on his last legs

I don't care to dance
I don't care to dance
I don't want to dance
I'm not going to dance

Angels twitch nervously
the brave and the bold weep
we all want to know who
we should pay tribute to

Hey good looker
you could tell me all about it
go on - tell me all about it
I know your secrets
you could tell me all about it
go on - tell me all about it

I may have lost the thread
I was supposed to pull
may I say everyone
is irresistible

Everyone is irresistible
now I'm not sure which way I should turn
I can say 'Now I've seen everything'
at last there must be no more to learn

That's what you want to hear
sadly, also it's true
and I know all your ways
and I'm still hung up on you

Oh great beautician in the sky
your innocence just saddens me
I shall throw it all against the wall
take my pleasure in spite of it all

I know your secrets
you could tell me all about it
go on - tell me all about it
hey good looker
I could fall all night all over you
hey good looker
roses are red, violets are blue

THE LIGHT POURS OUT OF ME

Time flies
time crawls
like an insect
up and down the walls

The light pours out of me
the light pours out of me

The conspiracy
of silence ought
to revolutionise
my thought

The light pours out of me
the light pours out of me

The cold light of day
pours out of me
leaving me black
and so healthy

The light pours out of me
the light pours out of me

It jerks out of me
like blood
in this still life
heart beats up love

The light pours out of me
the light pours out of me

PARADE

They will show me what I want to see
we will watch without grief
we stay one step ahead of relief
you tell me we've been praying
for a bright and clever hell
I think we've been forced to our knees but I can't tell

Sometimes I forget that we're supposed to be in love
sometimes I forget my position

It's so hot in here
what are they trying to hatch?
we must not be frail, we must watch
now that I'm out of touch with anger
now I have nothing to live up to
and I don't know when to stop joking
when I stop I hope I am with you

Sometimes I forget that we're supposed to be in love
sometimes I forget my position

What on earth is the size of my life?

MY MIND AIN'T SO OPEN

My mind
it ain't so open
that anything
could crawl right in
my mind
it ain't so open
that anything
could crawl right in
the last place
to lose yourself
is in the world
where we all cling

Oh my lover
we are opening
windows we see
all that we see
overlooking
our vivid room
is it such a
dumb thing to do?
my life
happens around me
your life
happens around me too

TOUCH AND GO

In the corner of your eye
I'm loitering with intent
you can tell me to move on
cos all my money's spent
you're such a big girl
small world, isn't it?
you ask me what I do
well sometimes I stand
and sometimes I sit

Then you tell me so
it's touch and go
for now
why must it be so?
we'll touch and go
oh wow

You live in a big story
a party to all kinds of things
innerventing excuses discovering new sins
you take a thousand liberties with me
saying "that's the price
for this kind of instant intimacy"

You strolled the pavements of a million dark hearts
flaunting your quality
patching up rows between fizgigs and demireps
you take your pleasures seriously

You offer me your hand
are you trying to catch something?
do you want to open me up?
do you want to close me in?

GIVE ME EVERYTHING

You're gonna give me immunity
you're gonna receive punishment
I'm gonna lose myself in you
because you're not quite of this world

There will be rooms
where we shouldn't meet
times I want to screw you up
and leave you in the street
you know everybody
you don't know a thing
you watch me in you
but I know what you're really seeing

With the eyes of the world upon you
you leave nothing to my imagination
and I leave nothing to be desired
cos you're gonna feel like I feel

Now you give me everything
now you give me everything
now you give me everything
now give me everything

And I'll open up like a sliding door
oh so oblique and easy
oh you're so bleak and easy
cos you're gonna feel like I feel

Now you give me everything
now you give me everything
now you give me everything
now give me everything

I beg of you
I beg of you
I beg of you

1978-79

FEED THE ENEMY

RHYTHM OF CRUELTY

CUT-OUT SHAPES

TALK TO THE BODY

I WANTED YOUR HEART

BELIEVE THAT I UNDERSTAND

BACK TO NATURE

PERMAFROST

TV BABY

FEED THE ENEMY

It's always raining over the border
there's been a plane crash out there
in the wheatfields
they're picking up the pieces
we could go and look
and stare

How many friends have we over there?
the border guards fight unconvincingly
whatever we do
it seems things are arranged
we always have to feed the enemy

You could dance for me
and punch me through
you could dance for me
and punch me through
dance for me

We watched them trash the last camera
glued to all of our TVs
the actors on the replay
trying again to touch you and me

But they always seem to know
exactly what they're talking about
now they've got you in a corner
you've got no room to move
you've got no room for doubt
that's exactly what they're talking about
now they've got you in a corner
no room to move
no room for doubt

RHYTHM OF CRUELTY

I brought your face down on my head
it was something I rehearsed in a dream
you're too goodlooking for your own damn good
and you don't know what it could mean

You've got me dying of thirst in the meantime
it even hurts when I scream
you've got me drowning and still in the meantime
you don't know what it could mean

Because in my drunken stupor
I've got to admire your ingenuity
and nod my head so wisely
to the rhythm of your cruelty

You're oh so anguished now
you're oh so anguished now
you've got me dying of thirst in the meantime
it even hurts when I scream
you've got me drowning and still in the meantime
you don't know what it could mean

Because you want to have your price
and something you could hold your faith up to
I don't know how to tell you this
but you've got it coming all the way to you

You don't know what it could mean
you don't know what it could mean
I don't know what it could mean
we don't know what it could mean

CUT-OUT SHAPES

I enter the room
confident enough
for now I tread
a straight and narrow way
so I sleep soundly
a little blue in the face
cut-out shapes
in secondhand daylight

Somewhere else
something else
on my mind

She's caressing me
with the hidden hands
of the only kind of violence
she thinks I'll understand
we've got them dancing
to all of our confessions
they don't know how
we rehearse our dreams

Somewhere else
something else
on my mind
I just get numb
when you're hard to find

We met at a psychiatric unit
she was in for having habits
no one else would try
she didn't know what she was in control of
she had all the advantages of magic
no one could deny

There was an old lady
who swallowed a fly
your inescapable mother
such a crazy lover

I just get numb
when you're hard to find
I just get numb
when you're hard to find

Find out
you'll find out

TALK TO THE BODY

You put me in the pictures
in the pictures in which my head is swimming
you were made for life
you're lost to the world
very transparent, very selfish
beautiful powerful careless women
watch it

My body screams yes
my mind just keeps its peace
clam up, calm down

We embrace during the journey
such a short ride in a borrowed car
the time is ripe for getting things right
at a very reminiscent temperature
watch it

My body screams yes
my mind just keeps its peace
clam up, calm down
clam up, calm down

I WANTED YOUR HEART

I wanted your heart
for the last time
I want to be in your bed
I want your words
to colour all that's been said
"I will love you when the devil is blind"
I wanted your heart
you didn't want mine

This is as close as I get
as I ever get
falling for things
I never thought
I'd find myself
falling for
as close as I get

Old ladies on the pavement
in the dense and empty hours
all as hard as nails
and brittle as pressed flowers
I was cold at an equally cold place
a cigarette between the flame and my face
you were laughing
like the goon squad in my heart
you were laughing
like the goon squad in my heart

This is as close as I get
as I ever get
falling for things
I never thought
I'd find myself
falling for
as close as I get

I wanted your heart
I wanted your heart

What do you think about
what I think about?
truths that are lies
when you spell them out
don't worry
don't betray the slightest emotion
yes I know
it's a separate emotion

As close as I get

BELIEVE THAT I UNDERSTAND

Here is the love of your life
once again, once again
here is the love of your life
once again, once again
she fits the part
she fills the space
she'll never ever be out of place
she's got it all with her saintly face
another sick monkey
with a saintly face
another sick monkey
with a saintly face

Here is the lie of the land
once again, once again
here is the lie of the land
once again, once again
you squeeze yourself
out of your thin inner world
you squeeze yourself
out of your thin inner world
you squeeze yourself
into the big wide world
it's all in the hands
of your very best friends
it's good to agree
with the good guys again

You win some
then you lose some
you win some
then you lose some
put it out of your mind
put it out of your mind
you should look at me

So tell me your troubles again
and again and again
tell yourself not to do it again
and again and again
you want to touch me
show me your hands
you want to touch me
show me your hands
you want to touch me
show me your hands
you'd better believe that I understand
you'd better believe that I understand

BACK TO NATURE

Back to nature
I can't go on like this
I want to walk where the power is
back to nature
I don't know where to start
back to nature
I don't have that kind of heart

Back to nature
back to somewhere else
back to nature
and right back on top of yourself
back to nature
I've got to look down
see where I am
or just hit the ground

And I'm telling you
I know what you've been going through
in my heart of hearts
when I was here
and you were there
nothing was between us

We're up in the air
we're down on the ground
we're up in the air
we're down on the ground

Here are your friends again
inching in the bedroom door
ah they want to touch me
and you show me their hands
how warm and soft and foreign they are
Cubans in surgical gloves
one on top of two on top of three
well I've got more than you

Back to nature
the voyeur will realise
this is not a sight for his sore eyes
back to nature
getting back at you
I couldn't act naturally if I wanted to

Back to nature
a trip that I can't take
people are thinking
that they've dreamed of this place
back to nature
it was somewhere else
back to nature
right back on top of yourself

And I'm telling you
I know what you've been going through
in my heart of hearts
when I was here
and you were there
nothing was between us

We're up in the air
we're down on the ground
we're up in the air
we're down on the ground

PERMAFROST

Thunder shook loose hail
on the outhouse again
today I bumped into you again
I have no idea what you want
but there was something I meant to say

As the day stops dead
at the place where we're lost
I will drug you and fuck you
on the permafrost

There's not much that I miss
I'm far too forgetful for that
sugar's sweet some of the time
it's hard to keep some things in mind

As the day stops dead
at the place where we're lost
I will drug you and fuck you
on the permafrost

TV BABY

TV baby
I don't know what to think
TV baby
I don't know what to think
my mind's on the blink
I don't know what to think
TV baby
I don't know what to think

TV baby TV baby TV baby TV baby
I'm taking the leap for you
taking the leap for you
I leap for you
leap for you leap for you

TV baby-oh
be looking out for you

1979-80

BECAUSE YOU'RE FRIGHTENED

MODEL WORKER

I'M A PARTY

YOU NEVER KNEW ME

PHILADELPHIA

I WANT TO BURN AGAIN

SWEETHEART CONTRACT

STUCK

A SONG FROM UNDER
THE FLOORBOARDS

TWENTY YEARS AGO

THE BOOK

UPSIDE DOWN

BECAUSE YOU'RE FRIGHTENED

You love me because you're frightened
and I'm falling in love with you
because I'm getting frightened
of the things you somehow make me do
you love me because you're frightened
I can easily believe my eyes
your fear is my finest hour
my fear is your disguise

Look what fear's done to my body
look what fear's done to my body

A frightening world
is an interesting world to be in
in the Forbidden City
or on The Roof of the World
or at the receiving end
of the nine o'clock news
however you put your mind to it
you can find fear where you choose

Look what fear's done to my body
look what fear's done to my body

You want to hurt
you want to crave
you want to praise and curse and blame
you want to believe just what you like
then you want to hurt and crave again

They took you to the top of the mountain
they showed you the valley
you bought it
you couldn't wait, could you?

Look what fear's done to my body
look what fear's done to my body

You want to hurt
you want to crave
you want to praise and curse and blame
you want to believe just what you like
then you want to hurt and crave again

You want to hurt and crave again
crave again

MODEL WORKER

I'm sick of working on the land
I wanna work with machines and look handsome

I have been indulging
in ostentatious display
doing little more than eat
three square meals a day

And I've been shirking my duty
so I've been sending gifts to curry favour

But because I love you
and because you love me
a model worker
I'll willingly be

I need a holiday, I've not been well
take me to the Brocade River Hotel

And I just want to know
while the revolution lasts
will it enable me
to swallow broken glass?

I'm not too worried by hegemony
I know the cadre will look after me

And I just want to know while the revolution lasts
will it enable me to swallow broken glass?

I have been indulging in ostentatious display
doing little more than eat three square meals a day

But because I love you and because you love me
a model worker I'll willingly be

A model worker
I'll willingly be

I'M A PARTY

I'm such and such
I'm a scream
bad choices take me to task
you'll see
I'll take out the car
but nobody'll want to crash

Take me with you
I'm a party
I don't know where I've been
so all things being equal
I'm a party
I won't know where we're going

You could do me a favour
do whatever you want to
I will let you hurt me
because I know it hurts you
it hurts you

What you say goes
I'm a party
all over the town
I fell into you
I keep up with all that's coming down

So, what's shaking?
I'm a party
you've got me racing, you've got me racing
the sound of a siren
in all the spaces between

You could do me a favour
do whatever you want to
I will let you hurt me
because I know it hurts you
it hurts you

I know it hurts you
I'm a party

YOU NEVER KNEW ME

I don't want to turn around
and find I'd got it wrong
or that I should have been laughing all along
you're what keeps me alive
you're what's destroying me
do you want the truth or do you want your sanity?

You were hell
and everything else was just a mess
I found I'd stepped into the deepest unhappiness
we get back
I bleed into you
thank God that I don't love you
all of that's behind me now
still seems to be above you

I don't know
I don't know whether I ever knew you
but I know you
I know you never knew me
I don't know
I don't know whether I ever knew you
but I know you
I know you never knew me

Do you want to?

Hope doesn't serve me now
I don't move fast at all these days
you think you've understood
you're ignorant that way
I'm sorry, I'm sorry, I'm sorry
I'm sorry I can't be cancelled out like this
we had to kill too much
before we could even kiss

I don't know
I don't know whether I ever knew you
but I know you
I know you never knew me
I don't know
I don't know whether I ever knew you
but I know you
I know you never knew me

Do you want to?

PHILADELPHIA

Your clean-living, clear-eyed
clever, level-headed brother says
he'll put all the screws
upon your newest lover
Buddha's in the fireplace
the truth's in drugs from Outer Space
maybe it's right to be nervous now

Who are these madmen?
what do they want from me?
with all of their straight-talk from their misery

Everything'd be just fine
if I had the right pastime
I'd've been Raskolnikov
but Mother Nature ripped me off
in Philadelphia
I'm sure that I felt healthier
maybe it's right to be nervous now

I had liberty of movement
but I'm so lazy
I'm so lazy
I'm just so lazy

You're just a big kid
you're not so big at that
you never got the hang of it
now you're being looked at

Where have I seen you before?
'Same place you saw me, I expect
I've got a good face for memories'
in Philadelphia
I'm sure that I felt healthier
maybe it's right to be nervous now

I WANT TO BURN AGAIN

The newcomer arrives
possession and guilt in his face
apologises to the Customs man
for the gaping hole in his suitcase
says 'I've seen where promises are made
I've seen how people are undone
it's always done
man to man
one to one'

I'm ditching an empty suitcase
I've been in Storytown
I've been swimming in poisons
been slowing up and down
I've known the eeriest wounds
the soul's long quarantine
when no rewards remain
no one and nothing comes clean

I've been blown about for years
on my way to you
I've been blown about for years
on my way to you
and I still turn to love
I want to burn again
and I still turn to love

In a room
where arrangements are made for success
you try to say that you possess me
by your caress
I met your lover yesterday
wearing some things I left at your place
singing a song that means a lot to me
I've known a certain grace

I've been blown about for years
on my way to you
I've been blown about for years
on my way to you
and I still turn to love
I want to burn again
and I still turn to love

I'm still turning
I want to burn again

SWEETHEART CONTRACT

We drank from cups on standard-issue sofas under scaffolding
informed sources said we were seen by observers - it's a meeting
I received an education
I was dominant for hours

I won myself a wealth of weapons, supermassive wealth
under a sweetheart contract which clearly stated
'Strength is always health'
I had one upper hand
I was dominant for hours

I want to be there, on the far side of sin
I've been putting myself through hell, waiting for hell to begin
I got insurance
I was dominant for hours

My tour-de-force is to forget all that's gone on around and about me
my manners are forever and whatever sells the newspapers suits me
I got an education
I was dominant for hours

I had one upper hand
I was dominant for hours

I got insurance
I was dominant for hours

We'd better give it back, it's not ours

STUCK

In the rush
the rush of my senses
in the heat
the heat of this moment
in the Palace of Nations
I think I can love you out of weakness

In the heat of this moment I stick myself in laughter

Run for it
I'm running away
know-it-all
I will return again
pushing myself so helpless
hopeless
when I can love you out of weakness

Which of us is to blame?
I'm stupid
I only know enough to get out of the rain

Oh, I really tiptoe, I really tiptoe

Stop
when you cease to amaze me
take a look
my part in the pattern
I know it'll never matter
so I stick myself in laughter

I may love you out of weakness
is that what I was afraid of?

A SONG FROM UNDER THE FLOORBOARDS

I am angry I am ill and I'm as ugly as sin
my irritability keeps me alive and kicking
I know the meaning of life, it doesn't help me a bit
I know beauty and I know a good thing when I see it

This is a song from under the floorboards
this is a song from where the wall is cracked
my force of habit, I am an insect
I have to confess I'm proud as hell of that fact

I know the highest and the best
I accord them all due respect
but the brightest jewel inside of me
glows with pleasure at my own stupidity

This is a song from under the floorboards
this is a song from where the wall is cracked
my force of habit, I am an insect
I have to confess I'm proud as hell of that fact

I used to make phantoms I could later chase
images of all that could be desired
then I got tired of counting all of these blessings
and then I just got tired

This is a song from under the floorboards
this is a song from where the wall is cracked
my force of habit, I am an insect
I have to confess I'm proud as hell of that fact

Habit

FOR F.D.

TWENTY YEARS AGO

You turn pandemonium
into pantomime for one
twenty years ago I used your soap

So what!
you've got a name for it
yesterday goes on and on
inbetween the devil and the deep blue sea

You thrash about in your room
no space for thought
look no strings, look no strings
no visible means of support

Twenty years ago I used your soap

How did you ever come to move a muscle in this space?

The dollar's adrift

Twenty years ago I used your soap

THE BOOK

This man is at the door of Hell...somehow it seems to be his destination after a life of subtle stubbornness. He doesn't expect to find himself waking up out of a dream...he doesn't expect to pinch himself and wake up and that kind of thing...in fact, the thought of that happening makes him smile. He's just mildly surprised to find himself there at the door of Hell.

To all accounts, the kindly old man who is the doorman (and who conceivably reminds him of his father) is sat reading a book...but he gets up smartly and without time for either of them to feel that they're standing on ceremony says, "Hold my book for a minute, would you, while I get the door open?" (Presumably, you know, you need two hands to open the door.) For some reason the old man doesn't just put his book down on the chair.

It all happens quite quickly...he finds that he's made a decision and is already holding the old man's book...as just about anybody else would have. But it seems a bit curious because...in however small a way you like to consider it...it is as if he's helping himself enter Hell...the path of least resistance. Of course, at the same time he suddenly thinks...even as he finally grips the book..."This is my chance for a reprieve...the final test...the straw which will tip the good deeds over the bad."

Next thing he knows, they have exchanged opinions on the book and he has handed it back to the old man and is being shown into Hell.

UPSIDE DOWN

I think of the distance
between you and me
which doesn't explain
why the strangest places
still call my name
I don't know how to live
I only know how to disappear
and I don't want to travel
and I don't want to stay here

They speak of destiny and fate
and powers that move unseen
and I get these pictures
of how my life might have been
I hear home is where the heart is
but I never get to learn
where my heart is

Upside down
upside down
I'm always turning things
upside down

The timing was right
but it was still a surprise
to find my heart had followed my eyes
I was just another man
with his eyes on you
and a need for agony
that he had to subdue

Upside down
upside down
I'm always turning things
upside down

in your eyes

1980-81

ABOUT THE WEATHER

SO LUCKY

THE HONEYMOON KILLERS

VIGILANCE

COME ALIVE

THE GREAT MAN'S SECRETS

THIS POISON

NAKED EYE

SUBURBAN RHONDA

THE GARDEN

IN THE DARK

THE OPERATIVE

ABOUT THE WEATHER

The weather's variable - so are you
changes, changes
but I can't do a thing about the weather
do you have your ticket?
can you foresee
changes, changes
another time when we might be together?

You have a broken window
through which the rain pours in my ear
this week's been all ears and edges
it's getting like a career

A chain of events
a change of heart
a chain of events
a change of heart

I will study your change of heart in depth

The weather's variable - so are you
changes, changes
but I can't do a thing about the weather
do you have your ticket?
can you foresee
changes, changes
another time when we might be together?

Now you're leaning on a fountain
with the sunshine on your shoes
you dislike the climate but you like the place
I hope you learn to live with what you choose

A chain of events
a change of heart
a chain of events
a change of heart

I will study your change of heart in depth

I'm so changeable - it's so frightening
I'm so changeable - it's so frightening

SO LUCKY

In this world of carelessness
there is delight, there is distress
a wilderness of mortal calm
sometimes ease, sometimes alarm

Lead me to a new world of comfort
lead me to a new world of comfort

Leave now quick, before you're missed
you can use the service lift
the neighbours're out on the morning shift
there needn't be the slightest risk

You know, we're lucky to be so important
you know, we're lucky it turned out that way
we are so lucky
we are so lucky

In this world of carelessness
there is delight, there is distress
we're never safe, that's for sure
the lucky shot through the open door

Lead me to a new world of comfort
lead me to a new world of comfort

So take your life in your hands and go
don't tell me where, I'd better not know
if I need to get in touch one day
I will employ the C.I.A.

Our love will equal the five year plan
like the harvest we'll cover the land
we are so lucky
we are so lucky

Lead me to a new world of comfort
lead me to a new world of comfort

THE HONEYMOON KILLERS

All police leave has been cancelled
we always imagine we're being followed

I saw an advert for ice cream
seems it was eaten in the Garden of Eden
I bought you one
you licked it slowly
and I got that certain feeling of freedom

Then we listened closely to some Mantovani
and waited for the cops to come

VIGILANCE

I'm in love with everything that's been left unsaid
that's gone down through the centuries
beginning
middle
and ending dead

I will forget
where I began
I'll lose track
I'll change hands
I'm not vigilant
it's no trouble
it's inevitable

It's so foggy at night always
and it's dark all day
all that has been hidden
will be shut off one day
until then I will attempt
whatever tempts me
tell me, is that good enough?
there's so much I can't see

I will forget
where I began
I'll lose track
I'll change hands
I'm not vigilant
it's no trouble
it's inevitable

You say in a little while
we'll have it all on file
my time ain't so vast
I can't spend it in the past

I will forget
where I began
I'll lose track
I'll change hands
I'm not vigilant
it's no trouble
it's inevitable

COME ALIVE

Bits of spirits were set on a carpet of carbon
pieces of apes were placed in a time of ice and iron

‘Keep fit - Survive’
‘Keep fit - Survive’

Primitive jeeps crushed fossils and ancient bone
chandelier-sized flowers aromatized pollen and chromosome
puzzles grew on trees where mutilated fruit hung
like the hats of inscrutable guests
who’d sipped their soft drinks and sung:

‘Keep fit - Survive’
‘Keep fit - Survive’
‘You won’t recognise yourself till you come alive’

Pepsi-Cola, Pepsi-Cola brings your ancestors back from the grave
Pepsi-Cola, Pepsi-Cola brings your ancestors back from the grave

At Leonardo da Vinci Intercontinental Airport
a Swiss pathologist missed his connecting flight

An asteroid kicked up the dust the dinosaur stubbornly bit
man’s brain was taken
the cortex stuck at an awkward angle on it
his first words were:

‘What have I done to deserve the sun?”
‘What have I done to deserve the rain?”

Pepsi-Cola, Pepsi-Cola brings your ancestors back from the grave
Pepsi-Cola, Pepsi-Cola brings your ancestors back from the grave

THE GREAT MAN'S SECRETS

Forget about law
forget the crowded will
order will do
men are so easy to kill

A house of mistakes
a blood-filled flame
bad blood in motion
no proof to blame

The great man's secrets
the great man's secrets
the great man's secrets
the great man's secrets

Daily your dream becomes more of a nightmare to me
but I learned more than a hundred ways to fall asleep
our terror seems to be vanity
progress is hard with madness around your feet

The great man's secrets
the great man's secrets
the great man's secrets
the great man's secrets

In years to come all of this will be
nothing more than mystery to me

I was moved from one cell to another

I will leave by the same door I came in

The great man's secrets
the great man's secrets
the great man's secrets
the great man's secrets

In years to come all of this will be
nothing more than mystery to me

I must confess
I must admit
my executioner hasn't changed a bit

THIS POISON

My lifetime's habits will remain
this crush of hearts won't go away
tonight, one way, once and for all
good times aren't possible today

I took a little poison
I took it carefully
it built for me
a house on fire
this poison takes after me

This poison came too far to fail
desire unwinds in the last hour
within, the bed is overturned
my host, the antidote is sour

I took a little poison
I took it carefully
it built for me
a house on fire
this poison takes after me

Now put me down upon the lawn
right here - next to my favourite tree
I'm being foolish - can't you tell?
they all look just the same to me

I took a little poison
I took it carefully
it built for me
a house on fire
this poison takes after me

NAKED EYE

She's wearing the shoes today
she's kicking her dog in the snow
she bought all three yesterday
she's the happiest person I know

When she's in a desert
when she's face to face with the sky
she can cast all the shadow she needs
with her naked eye

SUBURBAN RHONDA

You urban vision of loveliness
moving scenes of skin
you understand the ways and means
of city discipline
a structured life in some girls' rooms.
mirror glass and light
outside the landscape of power
dreams around appetites

Suburban Rhonda
don't be so smart
Suburban Rhonda
don't act so sharp
Suburban Rhonda
you'll wreck your heart
Suburban Rhonda
you'll wreck your heart

You could be just vain and live alone
on Separation Street
but if you did you know your life
would be incomplete
the tenements of disrepute
don't eye them longingly
I want to be the one
to put you out of your misery

Suburban Rhonda
don't be so smart
Suburban Rhonda
don't act so sharp
Suburban Rhonda
you'll wreck your heart
Suburban Rhonda
you'll wreck your heart

You'll wreck your heart

THE GARDEN

I'm in a web
I TASTED BLOOD IN THE GARDEN
I'm in a maze, I'm in a maze
SO THEY HUNG SCIENCE IN MY HEART
I'm in a web
"YOUR PHONEY GHOSTS WENT BY" I LAUGHED
I'm in a maze, I'm in a maze
"I DRAGGED THEM OUT OF THE DARK"

I'm open wide
I PRESSED THORNS INTO MY FLESH
I am awake, I am awake
MY EYES LOOK LIKE CLAWS
I'm open wide
MAN EATING MAN EATING MAN
I am awake, I am awake
MY SICKNESS IS MY REWARD

I'm in a web
I'D SWEAR I SAW THE SUNLIGHT SHAKE
I'm in a maze, I'm in a maze
THE SKY'S ALL OVER MY HEAD
I'm in a web
I'M FEELING GRAVITY HARDEN
I'm in a maze, I'm in a maze
SOUNDING THE ALARM FROM THE CENTRE OF A FLOWERBED

I'm open wide
I AM THE ONLY ONE AWAKE
I am awake, I am awake
AND I'M SO WELL INFORMED
I'm open wide
I'LL SEE THE BOTTOM OF THE LAKE
I am awake, I am awake
IN THE EYE OF A BRAINSTORM

I AM RESPONSIBLE
I AM RESPONSIBLE
man eating man eating man
I AM RESPONSIBLE
I AM RESPONSIBLE

IN THE DARK

Keep it in the dark
you say now you want to stay

Put on your clothes
I think you should go away

I can lose my way on the shortest of journeys

Keep it in the dark
there is no defeating it

Put on your clothes
or I'm not eating it

I can lose my way on the shortest of journeys

THE OPERATIVE

You were never found to be backward
or wanting in any way
you were hidden so cleverly in love
what scheme did you obey?

And I know why you go so slow
and I know why you go so slow
and I know why you go so slow

You had such strange disappointments
too bare against the paint
you knew the handle was broken
and your strong arm was faint

And I know why you go so slow
and I know why you go so slow
and I know why you go so slow

Your tired empire's fallen
victim to your unease
you could make yourself so useful
if you'd get on your knees

And I know why you go so slow
and I know why you go so slow
and I know why you go so slow

1982-83

COLD IMAGINATION

TOPLESS

RAINY SEASON

I ADMIRE YOU

WAY OUT OF SHAPE

SOME WILL PAY
FOR WHAT OTHERS PAY TO AVOID

WAITING FOR A TRAIN

OUT OF SHAPE WITH ME

TAKING OVER HEAVEN

SEEING IS BELIEVING

WITHOUT LEAVING

DEAL OF THE CENTURY

THE CONVENTION

COLD IMAGINATION

Hey, I'm freezing
I can't give in an inch
am I dreaming?
did I feel a pinch?

Hey, I'm freezing
icicles are on the vine
this ice age
it could finish off Frankenstein

Sheets of ice over every machine
from election day to Hallowe'en
am I acting badly in some bad dream?
please pull me out of this Arctic ditch
crush the winter, throw the switch
burn my ticket to the satellite fridge

Get me out of my cold imagination
get me out of my cold imagination
let me out
I've got a cold imagination
through and through

Hey, I'm freezing
no news of a thaw
I don't know
anyone I telephone anymore

Hey, I'm freezing
I can't give into you one inch
I'm freezing
did I dream I felt a pinch?

An avalanche buries the bridge
while scornful eyes on a windswept ridge
peer down at me in cold storage
but underneath this everlasting frost
the best will in the world is lost
his fingers too cold to count the cost

Get me out of my cold imagination
get me out of my cold imagination
let me out
I've got a cold imagination
through and through

TOPLESS

The past is rotten to the core
the time is ripe like never before
it's so normal
I'm not entertaining doubt
I'm let off the hook and out

All for nothing
you call me topless
you call me incomplete
all for nothing
you call me topless
you call me incomplete
and I love you like no one else

Into your service I am home
where I can take unto myself my own
your beauty's making me seem free
it's only normal
there's never been any choice for me

It takes all sorts
you are perfect
you can do no wrong
it takes all sorts
you are perfect
you make me feel like Napoleon
and I love you like no one else
and I love you like no one else

I love you like no one else
I love you like no one else

RAINY SEASON

Was it really only yesterday
when you left in such a rush
and the falling cliffs filled the bay?
I used to know this place
I used to know your name
my skin remembers

I am on fire
and it's the rainy season
in this desert
you made me create
I am on fire
and it's the rainy season
and you're like a mirage
I could learn to hate

The future's missing here
on some coral reef
you called me all the names
under the sun
in your sleep
stirring the blue-grey waves
I'm steady as she goes
my brain's a leaky boat
my brain's a leaky boat

I am on fire
and it's the rainy season
in this desert
you made me create
I am on fire
and it's the rainy season
and you're like a mirage
I could learn to hate

You had broken my heart already
I'd just seen you across the room
I made up my mind
five feet into the flames
to pray for the break of the monsoon

I pray for the break of the monsoon

I think I'm coming down with something new
I'm running errands for your friends I hardly know
I used to know this place
I used to know your name
my skin remembers

I am on fire
and it's the rainy season
in this desert
you made me create
I am on fire
and it's the rainy season
and you're like a mirage
I could learn to hate

I ADMIRE YOU

My natural enemies
they don't want me
to go on loving you
I'm nonplussed

Now I'm past caring
for what they have to say
I see things your way
because I must

Because I admire you
because I desire you
because I require you
forever
for everyone

Just keep this paradise
between you and me
an excellent mystery
to consume

And rain is unremembered here
nothing else to reverse
for better, for worse
we're immune

Because I admire you
because I desire you
because I require you
forever
for everyone

This is what I'm up against
when I am with you
it's driving me to distraction
I must be loving you
to the very edge
of my very own satisfaction

Because I admire you
because I desire you
because I require you
forever
for everyone

I admire you
I have done all along
I desire you
forever and everyone

WAY OUT OF SHAPE

I am upon the sofa
inhaling especially slow
you lean hard on the fridge
you're feeling so low

I've got a roof over my head
you've got a gun in my back
I get to cower behind the curtains
but I never unpack

Come and be
out of shape with me
come and be
deflected out of tragedy

Here is positive identification
it's just one of those days
when I might as well be drunk
cos I can do it every other way

Come and be
out of shape with me
come and be
deflected out of tragedy

It's all up in the air
it's all going the way of the kitchen sink
and there's only one thing certain
I'd like another drink

But I'll give it everything
everything I've been given
I know I'm way out of line
but I'm stumbling into heaven

Come and be
out of shape with me
come and be
deflected out of tragedy

Once upon a time
everything was promised to me
and I walked down the line...

SOME WILL PAY
FOR WHAT OTHERS PAY TO AVOID

What are you going to do?
the time has come and I have forgiven you
I don't know
I don't think so

Some will pay for what others pay to avoid

It's just a matter of time
oh how my memories press us together
and the dream is catching up

Some will pay for what others pay to avoid

According to these memories
I'm just mad about you
I'm just mad about you
our jerky versions of The Dream
made it all seem so true
made it all seem so true

Because I was naked I was afraid
to have my feelings displayed
but now it's come to this
I will deliberately miss you

Some will pay for what others pay to avoid

And I gave in to temptation
God forbid, God forbid

According to these memories
I'm just mad about you
I'm just mad about you
our jerky versions of The Dream
made it all seem so true
made it all seem so true

Rise up to me
from the bottom of my heart
and come back to me

I gave in to temptation, God forbid
it was simply the best thing I ever did
I gave in
I caved in

WAITING FOR A TRAIN

Business hours are over now
I'm watching it get dark over the railway tracks
and I'm under a poster for painkiller comfort
shopping by camerawork
and trying to relax

And the wind turns in the air
I'm just waiting for the train
I'm feeling so good it cannot be fair
because tonight I'm seeing you again
tonight I'm seeing you again

I used to find myself
at the bitter end of remarkable occurrences

Yes, once upon a terrible time of my life
I was up, accused of GBM
grievous bodily mistakes
and trashy dreams
your honour, I can't even bear to think about them

Now there's been a reprieve
and I'm just waiting for this train
I'm finding it just a little hard to breathe
because tonight I'm seeing you again
tonight I'm seeing you again

So far, far, far along the platform
I'm a man with a problem and a request
mister, I shouldn't be here
get me a diesel
I assure you, it's in the national interest

And the wind turns in the air
I'm just waiting for the train
I'm feeling so good it cannot be fair
because tonight I'm seeing you again
tonight I'm seeing you again

I'm seeing you again
now I know what it is to be alive

Hello

OUT OF SHAPE WITH ME

I am upon the sofa
inhaling deliberately slow
you lean on the fridge
you're feeling so low

It's all up in the air
it's going the way of the kitchen sink
there's only one thing certain
I'd like another drink

I've got positive identification
yes - it's one of those days
I'm drunk, yes, I'm drunk
but I think I can do it okay

Come and be
out of shape with me
come and be
deflected out of this tragedy

Consider my delicate health for a moment

Have I given the game away?
I'm ailing and I can't escape
my name's missing from the active list
no way am I in useful shape

I'll give it everything
everything I've been given
I know I'm way out of line
hope I'll stumble over heaven

Come and be
out of shape with me
come and be
deflected out of this tragedy

Have you heard, we're taking over heaven
some things'll have to go
some things'll have to be forbidden
I know like I know the back of my hand
there's gonna be the devil to pay
on demand

The clouds'll be white
the sky'll be blue
keep it under wraps
don't go taking naps

You've been knocking what you need
your unhappiness is guaranteed

Heads're gonna roll like there's no tomorrow
we'll be throwing up our hands in desperation and horror
YOU'RE AT THE MERCY OF SOMEONE WHO AIN'T THE BOSS
but I know he has feelings
WELL, THEY DON'T COME ACROSS

The clouds'll be white
the sky'll be blue
keep it under wraps
no taking naps

You've been knocking what you need
WE'RE TAKING OVER
Your unhappiness is guaranteed

Are we somebody else's angels?

Misfortune slept undisturbed for years in fits and starts
our good behaviour must've pulled out all the stops on his heart
we had voices before we had anything to say
you've still a tongue in your head now
so let us pray

The clouds will be white and the sky will be blue

WE'RE TAKING OVER
You've been knocking what you need
unhappiness is guaranteed
WE'RE TAKING OVER
we're taking over, taking over now
WE'RE TAKING OVER

SEEING IS BELIEVING

It's morning
and you're turning over
a new leaf you found in the undergrowth
I don't know why some things bother to change
I don't know, it's not a very interesting hoax

But seeing is believing is making do
seeing is believing is making do
so look around, look around
see what you find
I may have been overpowered and undermined

With these things that are about to happen
and yet, they're not
ah, well, it keeps me from getting in trouble
when I'm at my local beauty spot

Where seeing is believing is making do
seeing is believing is making do
so look around, look around
see what you find
I may have been overpowered and undermined

WITHOUT LEAVING

When I hit on love
with nothing to back it up
count me out of luck

Forgive me if I don't get up

Forgive me if I don't get up
forgive me if my numbers don't show
I'm always aiming to go

Count me out
I'm too naive
for too long I've been absent without leaving
I go missing out awkward scenes
daydreaming with a vengeance
supreme

I think she knows, I think she knows

"He's got a skullful
or kerosene and shortcuts
balanced on his neck
overhead, a jet
full of passengers
slumbering in his ear
she's weirder, weirder, weirder
than at any other time
she's got his chassis
nuzzling a foggy bottomline"

1. You're tempting fate away with this simple threat
"When you take chances sometimes chances are what you get"
then you said something to me
2. Then make your move
1. I don't quite know why, I was taken aback
2. Things will improve
1. "What you cannot carry you must drag and drag..."
2. Then make your move
3. It's exactly what I want!
2. Things will improve
3. It's exactly what I want!
1. "... drag and drag"
Le marché du siècle dans ton salon
2. Then make your move
3. It only looks as if it hurts
it's exactly what I want!
it's exactly what I want!
oh, it's exactly what I want!
1. How still you and I've made this place
how still you and I've made this place
then you said something to me
2. Then make your move
1. I don't quite know why, I was taken aback
2. Things will improve
1. "What you cannot carry you must drag and drag..."
2. Then make your move
3. It's exactly what I want!
2. Things will improve
3. It's exactly what I want!
1. "...drag and drag"
Your system of happiness has mastered me
2. Then make your move
3. It only looks as if it hurts
4. My first impulse was to buy it

THE CONVENTION

I've been looking at
all the candidates' wives
you're the loveliest
object of worship

All the broken hours
I'm going to mend
all the broken hours
in my grip

And if it's him you love
then I'm like him
I'll do my level best
I'm bound to say
I'm bound to say

If I were you
I'd distrust their every motive
I'm floating the company

I got the money
up in the mountains
it seems so human to me

And if it's him you love
then I'm like him
I'll do my level best
I'm bound to say
I'm bound to say

Lust in a ditch anyway

I've been looking at
all the candidates' wives
you're the loveliest
of them all

All the broken hours
I'm going to mend
all the broken hours
I can recall

Leave with me

1986-88

REDNECK

It's opening night
let's give them their money's worth
may this show run and run
till it falls off the edge of the earth
put on your make-up
powder puff adder of mine
dusk is upon us
switch on that shining sign

I am a major prophet
I'm heaven and hell bent strong
I am the height of a sign
wide of the mark
deep as the Amazon

I must impress on them
this opportunity
it'll be too late
by the time they put me on TV
I feel sharp
I feel blunt
a precision instrument
I really gleam
watch me bite on a bullet
and spit out a limousine

I am a major prophet
I'm heaven and hell bent strong
I am the height of a sign
wide of the mark
deep as the Amazon

Feel my wild sadness blowing down
feel my wild sadness blowing
all the way down

I stand before you
in full possession of the facts
I make no use of effects
no use for clever counterbalancing acts
I've broken every bone of meaning
in this body and this soul
I've bought knowledge
at the cost of a complete loss of self-control

All the truth you can bear
is yours to take away tonight
- the longer you leave it
- the more there's to leave
like you, I once saw
those pretty colours in black and white
- you've got to get it over with
- stop being naive
strangers to truth and to fiction
you will remain
- if I meet you at the fountainhead
- I'll win you downstream
walk away if you like
you've only yourself to blame
- I'm not talking eyewash
- I'm talking strychnine

I am a major prophet
I'm heaven and hell bent strong
I am the height of a sign
wide of the mark
deep as the Amazon

And I simply may be evil
I simply may be evil

FLESH

By the Egyptian Gate
I wait in my penance vest
I've never been so lost before
so I-can't-help-myself-possessed
I want to be torn through
the material of your flesh

Your husband lies unconscious
on Samuda's precipice
I drink in the dead night air
and your astringent kiss

She's slovenly lovely
he's a moth over opium
so long time stone cold sober
now marked down for delirium
her perfume draws his blood out
and back to this asylum slum

One man, one woman
walk around Newington Green
the worst case of resemblance
in N16

I hate having to desire you
hate feeling this again
I hate having to desire you
in common with other men

My fellow-creature-gods look out
to be mutually blessed
this therapeutic age leaves them cold
so fashionably distressed
but I just want to be torn through
the material of your flesh

"Cheer up, it'll never happen" they said
"not every candle burns
lighting up these lonely nights
in this century of germs
so ... many ... happy ... returns"

"Cheer up it'll never happen" they said
"we're here on your behalf"
"It already has" I said
they evaporate and laugh

I hate having to desire you
hate feeling this again
I hate having to desire you
in common with other men

The best in life
it's nothing special
remember who said it
our lives are running
oh my little death
this is forever
the final edit

PUBLIC HIGHWAY

I am the public highway, baby
I'm no place for pretence or protocol
I could take you
by way of a garden city
I could run you along
the Libido del Sol

I am this street now
I am the street where you live
see me from your window
and be a fugitive

Back of beyond the horizon
I cut and stretch
the outer space of open air
if there's somewhere
you just have to be, babe
oh let me be your thoroughfare

I am this street now
I am the street where you live
see me from your window
and be a fugitive

There is a pale swamp
a glacier
waxy crystal car
and the smell of woodsmoke
is on the evening breeze
and your engine's humming
like a pleasureboat
in the distance of the heat
tearing the blossom off the trees

We pass by Père Lachaise
and broken fences
we pass hospitals
in the San Fernando Valley
and all of my tricks
and turns and inclinations
you can't find them in your Rand McNally

LIVE NOW - live a thousand other lives
LIVE NOW - and learn the secret names of time
LIVE NOW - all at once and forever
LIVE NOW - and you'll be all mine

I am this street now
I am the street where you live
see me from your window
and be a fugitive

LADY 21

I was thinking of phoning
the richest woman in the town
a radio was playing nonsense
and yes,
the cigarette machine is broken down
watch yourself now
the lino's greasy
it could surely kill
ever since they fixed the light in here
this place has gone downhill

And now I'm running
up the aisle
of an endless train
and when I try to sleep
I dream the very same
I am nothing
becoming nothing
and nothing's to be done
then I'm falling in love
with Lady 21

Press me to her tumbling beauty
oh gorgeous siren wraith
I may never know what hit me
but I'll leap with all of my faith
I'll have her way with me
and be delivered as it occurs
she'll be smiling so happily
I'll break my body on hers
I'll break my body on hers

Put out the fetch-candle
if you're coming through
and be my familiar spirit
if you want to
deliver me unto my desire
deliver me unto my desire
I'm up on the heights
I'm still up on the heights

POUND

Can you put a price upon
every lingering breath
can you work it out and say
what every minute's worth
time is always money
and you're such a very heavy spender
you're squeaky clean
you're out of legal tender
then ...

Certainty
it's so sexy
you're too cold to drop
you could be eating
Ciba Geigy goat cheese
you need to tell someone
to tell you when to stop

There's only ever been
one soft option
one blank cheque
one deep breath
to take you up to the neck
you need more
I'll get you some
see me okay
with Rimbaud bubblegum

So much goes to Sally
so much goes to Mack & Nicholas
you'll get back your money
when the sublime
meets the ridiculous
bewitchingly ridiculous

You put your money where your mouth is
your balance is astounding
you're in for every penny
you're in for every pounding

Look at you now
powdered
pounding
now you're shilling
out for any count

any killing
you listen to the hours of your fingers flip flop
you need a franchise
Yamaha soda pop

What's that funny smell?
why aren't you out earning?
gimme your pittance, boy
the holes in your pockets
they're burning
I smell them burning

You put your money where your mouth is
and you can talk till doomsday
you can't take it with you, son
the hours of your fingers
tap on an empty urn
unless you let things take forever
they never get done
unless you let things take forever
they never get done

This is what I mean by my money
this is what I mean by my money

You put your money where your mouth is
and you can talk till doomsday
you can't take it with you, son
the hours of your fingers
tap on an empty urn
unless you let things take forever
they never get done

The real cost of living
it's changing all the time
don't set the clocks
against me again
hard luck
hard cash
but no hard feelings
I must dash
I have my feelings
I just can't say exactly when
I just can't say exactly when

CELEBRITY

I turned to her and I said

We'll hurl my biography
into this whirling pool
see which way the blue ink runs
on an ocean of lenses
I'm drifting like a fool
smouldering focus of those instant suns

And all of these
cause and effect motion pictures
impossible to avoid
a single image of me
it's living
on a whole subcontinent of celluloid

You'll like me
you're like me
you'll recognise my name
you'll like me
you're like me
have a picture of me
pointing out of frame
now go ...

The magnifying circus
the magnifying circus
a wealth of detail is going cheap
cause and error
trial and effect
isn't it enough to put you all to sleep?

But my likeness
it's to your liking
so I won't stay away
I'll be back long before you know it
to dazzle you again
I daresay

You'll like me
you're like me
you'll turn the page and watch
your kids are eating effigies of me
fluorescent butterscotch

There's a shimmering lake of real lives
it's a backdrop
it's an afterthought
tell me, will there be a dressing room
and will there be shadows at the airport?

This set is hotter than the Holy Land
it all beats down from above
long golden weeks of close-ups
cool and convincing shows of love

You'll like me
you're like me
you'll recognise my name
you'll like me
you're like me
have a picture of me
pointing out of frame

You'll like me
you're like me
you'll turn the page and watch
your kids are eating effigies of me
fluorescent butterscotch

If one life has been saved
by this photography session
it has been worth it

MLLE

*"Ces quelques pas du palier à la chambre d'Albertine, ces quelques pas que personne ne pouvait plus arrêter, je les fis avec délices, avec prudence, comme plongé dans un élément nouveau, comme si en avançant j'avais lentement déplacé du bonheur, et en même temps avec un sentiment inconnu de toute-puissance, et d'entrer enfin dans un héritage qui m'eût de tout temps appartenu."**

A winter's night
the Northern Quay
the Isle of Dogs
the rabid one is me
you sip your drink
undismayed
and I just said
"These days my heart seems to be a kind of hand grenade"

Nothing in the air tugs at the tower blocks
as you raise your finger and pull the pin
nothing much on earth moves down these desolating docks
do you really think you just scratched your chin?

But you were never Albertine
and I was never poor Marcel
who were you that time round,
Mademoiselle?

Monsieur a peur du parfum des princesses

And now I act up
and you've a winning frown
I've contracted love
as I'm devoured down
blame my deadening intensity
and tell me how you got the part in this
my own illicit agony

I lay it on pretty thick
you spread yourself pretty thin
ducking and dividing under every skin
and my final words as you get up and leave
"If you're free as air, I don't want to breathe"

Good evening,
I am the madman in love with your daughter
we need to talk
just you and me
I saw her last in Eden
or some other Far Eastern quarter
where the river snakes its way out to sea

But you were never Albertine
and I was never poor Marcel
who were you that time round,
Mademoiselle?

* Marcel Proust - A L'Ombre des Jeunes Filles en Fleurs

Those few steps from the landing to Albertine's door, those few steps which no one now could prevent my taking, I took with delight, with prudence, as though plunged into a new and strange element, as if in going forward I had been gently displacing the liquid stream of happiness, and at the same time with a strange feeling of absolute power, and of entering at length into an inheritance which had belonged to me from all time.

Translated by C K Scott Moncrieff

RUBBISH

Oh I leave to you
the rubbish of my love
oh my sunken love

I leave to you
the rubbish of my love
my nyktomorphic love

Today I bury my love alive
today I bury my love alive

I bury my love alive
under the rubble of my estate
I bury my love alive
under the rubble of my estate

And she gained on me
as I gave up
in the distance
out of sight
down a valley
where mist was hanging
in a pink and a golden light

In a pink and golden light
I bury my love alive
under the rubble of my estate

She said
"We could try getting lonely
on an altogether higher spiritual plane"
I said
"If it's all the same to you
I can't be bothered with that again"

Oh I leave to you
the rubbish of my love
oh my sunken love

Oh I leave to you
the rubbish of my love
my nyktomorphic love

Today I bury my love alive

We sleep in the city of dreams
we have settled under the dust
we take 40,000 winks
on the threshold of
unanswerable lust

God's gone back to heaven
he's deserted us
but what the hell
he never understood us anyway

Have our souls pined away?
have we sowed our seed in vain?
has he set his face against us
and now shall we be slain?
this is the Stone Age of our desire
these are our formative years
don't let them say the devil
slaked his raging thirst
on our filthy tears

God's gone back to heaven
he's deserted us
but what the hell
he never understood us anyway

We simply may be evil
I don't care if it's true
we simply may be evil
I don't care if it's true
I'm going to try anything, try anything
because I really want you
I've got to have everything, have everything
because I really really need to

God's gone back to heaven
he's deserted us
but what the hell
he never understood us anyway

SICKLY THUG & I

We're deep in her diary now
a month for every kiss
and this passion-in-hours amounts
to little more than this
she keeps wisteria
I keep forgetting to die

We keep on getting there
sickly thug and I
she keeps a distance
I keep forgetting to die
we'll keep on getting there
sickly thug and me
she keeps wisteria
I keep turning to lapis lazuli

A pistol whipping wind
sickly thug and me
our hearts fire blanks
over the marshes
the River Lee
was there anything
really moving in the news tonight?

If there's no hope for us
there'll be no respite
just a drop or two
from a bottle of the widow's mite
we'll keep on getting there
I'll just happen to you
we'll be back from somewhere else
we'll never get to

Over here may be bad
realissimo bad
but that nameless other place
it's far far worse
I'm an innocent
I never resisted
alcohol and coloured beads

Broken sunshine swells
the length of Waltham beach
and nothing ever changes
and nothing ever lasts for long
it just stays out of reach
this feeling's mutual
for sickly thug and me

This feeling's mutual now
but so separately
we're burning up
we're collapsing into probability
and there's no hope for us
and there's no respite
just a drop or two
from a bottle of the widow's mite

1988-90

THE BEAST BOX IS DREAMING

STUPID BLOOD

AGAINST THE PAST

OUR CURIOUS LEADER

WE KEEP ON GETTING THERE

TICKET

ANIMAL IN THE MIRROR

DIRTY BEATING HEART

SMOKING MIRROR

I'VE BEEN EXPECTING YOU

KAREZZA

BEAST BOX

USELESS LOVE

THE BEAST BOX IS DREAMING

Its shape tells us plainly
time inside is curved
it holds Elvis Presley's body
perfectly preserved

When Kennedy came with Monroe
late in '55
the senator carved their names
by the overdrive
it's an accident of nature
designed by architects
NASA built it from an alloy
they'd stolen from the Czechs

The Beast Box is dreaming
what you believe

The replica at Disneyland
in the big exhibition hall
it's correct to the last nut and bolt
it's nothing like it at all
if a pregnant woman touches it
the child will be shy
and if you glimpse it once
you eventually die

The Beast Box is dreaming
what you believe

In a dream I'm inside
with my kid brother
there's scenes of awful suffering
we're avoiding looking at each other
then he's pointing to the handrail
it's long, of burnished chrome
saying in that stupid voice of his
"Some of this would look good
in the bathroom back home"

Freemasons talk about it all the time
their hands at funny angles
in moonlight it resembles
a biscuit tin that dangles

The Beast Box is dreaming
what you believe

Juice in the front
juice in the back
a cardboard gothic frame
they sold it off for scrap last year
to our eternal shame

STUPID BLOOD

That, I'm afraid
and I'm not afraid
is that
why cut it fine
in a ludicrous hat
my prick
my very spirit?

My prick
my very spirit
my very stupid blood
once lit the slow dynamite of habit
for the genius of love

Burn your bridges
burn your boats
smell the life you never had
why cut it fine
in a ludicrous hat?

Burn your bridges
burn your boats
smell the life you never had
that, I'm afraid
and I'm not afraid
is that

AGAINST THE PAST

Candice Morganauer's gone to join
the quick and the dead clever
tonight we're seeing her final film
her crowning endeavour
she washed herself for years
in mouthwatering praise
but we all know she never grew up
she just shrank sideways

Yesterday was fine, I've forgotten it somehow
last week wouldn't even show up on radar now
last week wouldn't even show up on radar now

Winnie the Obscure
he's weighing his own heart
he's been sleeping like Calvin Coolidge
to keep himself apart
and now he's crying
"Old Drella is dead, and I didn't feel a thing"
and Jude the Pooh with a landslide smile replies
"All the more power to him"

Under the roofs and the gutters up above
even the sparrows are burning up with human love
even the sparrows are burning up with human love

Night of light
it's failing over Gringley-On-The-Hill
powders are on the plantation wind
over Dallowgill
we reach the doors to the doubtful city
they close as if in pain
out on Howard Devoto Boulevard
I remember you and me
we're kissing in the rain

And it's all so gone
and this could never last
I'll stay with you
I'll stay with you
against the past

It's gone
it could never last
I'll stay with you
I'll stay with you
against the past

OUR CURIOUS LEADER

Our curious leader knows what's best
how we're signalbound now to existential sex
our curious leader has such a lovely daughter
we wash their feet and quench our thirst with the same water

Our curious leader, he's never there
he's playing second fiddle to sumptuous despair
our curious leader is covered in deep sin
and when I grow up you know I want to be like him

Our curious leader reads every dream
in the church of man and bomb and beast and TV and machine
the usual angels will add to your failures
stand up, be counted, Buy Bailey's Trailers

Our curious leader has ransacked the loft
he's under the impression we have all gone soft
our curious leader has emptied the larder
pain is tough going but happiness is harder

WE KEEP ON GETTING THERE

We keep on getting there
we'll keep on until we do
I wouldn't hold my breath
if I were you
right now this could be anywhere

We keep on getting there
will we never arrive?
and if we ever do
will we still be alive?
they say we're beyond repair
we keep on getting there
we keep on getting there

We keep on getting there
our nerves always raw
as it was long ago
we've been here before
never, never again we swear

We keep on getting there
the tribe time forgot
we can hardly wait
whether we want to or not
you'll never catch us unaware
we keep on getting there
we keep on getting there

We keep on getting there
we're going with the flow
for the likes of us
there's nowhere else to go
we keep on getting there
there's no going back
we move from sign to sign
ahead of attack

On a withered wing
with a one word prayer
it's more than
I thought I could ever bear
we keep on getting there
we keep on getting there
we keep on

TICKET

Brutal bimbo beauty
nonsensically sublime
this hammy armageddon
turns out to be yours and mine
your face is just the ticket to everything
I ever wanted to see
your face is just the ticket to everything
I was ever required to be

Sweet subtle nothing
flower of my will
your physical beauty
is making me physically ill
I turn up again
fantastically resplendent
they pack them in to the hilt
funny thing is
the theatre hasn't even been built

I was up to absolute beauty
playing it by my own book
where there's no justice
in matters of beauty
it's stupid to even look
but I held on to my ticket
I'd sit in front of it and stare
have pity on me
I've still got it somewhere

ANIMAL IN THE MIRROR

You keep forgetting the lines
the lines that show
where you were bound
long ago
animal in the mirror
live out another mise en scène
somebody else's summer again
animal in the mirror
and stop this pretending
there's plenty of time
all your happy endings
will they never find
animal in the mirror?

Excited night
flickering trade
a bag of nerves
on a balustrade
animal in the mirror
slow dissolve in tears
tears that chart
how we're the same
the same worlds apart
animal in the mirror
and stop this pretending
there's plenty of time
all your happy endings
will they never find
animal in the mirror?

Oh Lord I spoke up this morning
I had nothing to say
above the hum of another
raw and exquisite day
Lord I broke up this morning
I rose in pieces and dreams
I was running late and scared
in Paris
in springtime
and fog juice streams

Forget your lines
the lines that show
where you were bound
long ago
animal in the mirror
slow dissolve
in tears that chart
how we're the same
the same worlds apart
animal in the mirror
after a fashion
after a fall
after reality
after all
animal in the mirror
stop this pretending
there's plenty of time
all your happy endings
will they never find
animal in the mirror?

DIRTY BEATING HEART

I copy love really badly
more often than not
all too little I've wanted
an awful lot
so I keep blowing you up
you keep coming apart
it's this dirty big, dirty great
dirty beating heart

Dirty beating heart
I love my love for you
dirty beating heart
string me along
dirty beating heart
you are like naked cable
you're stale, unstable
dirty beating heart
my carousel

I'm on the trail of vapours
down a fancy colonnade
where ghosts of stories parade
accept this wanton homage
I love my love for you
I am falling off a mountain without a view

Dirty beating heart
I love my love for you
dirty beating heart
string me along
dirty beating heart
you are like naked cable
you're stale, unstable
dirty beating heart
my carousel

Dirty beating heart
I really need to carry on
dirty beating heart
I know all too well
dirty beating heart
wanton homage
it's given gladly
you copy love so badly
dirty beating heart
how you string me along

Dirty beating heart
my dirty beating heart
love my dirty beating dirty beating
dirty beating dirty beating heart

SMOKING MIRROR

The window is wobbling
rain no doubt
four part water
one part poison
I really could do without

You can have my Picasso
please lie down
your funerary nakedness remains
under your successful dress and gown

Look in the smoking mirror
you're a thinking flame
into your silence
I'll introduce straight rain

From bergamot to tonka
on a sea breeze of turpentine
a sulphur rose with hammer-dressed eyes
a little light upstairs

At a slumber party poorly lit
a vaseline moon and would-be gems
you sleep on it
you're blinding me with rescue flares

You can have my Picasso
please lie down
your funerary nakedness remains
under your successful dress and gown

I'VE BEEN EXPECTING YOU

A massive moon
a jumped-up ape
I kiss the earth and choke
and make it to Gatwick
with a drill
and ten red roses
I slip and fall
a bananaskin
break out my heart
only waving
this night's fine
and all is fair
in love
and the war within me raging
you kill me off in theory
then you pardon me for breathing
the sweet smell of the street
it was so forgiving

I threw everything at you
my misery, my joy and truth
my haemorrhaging time
you probably don't remember me
et in Arcadia ego
my feelings did so very much for you

I threw nearly everything at you
my misery, my joy and truth
my haemorrhaging time
and my piecemeal grief
and all I was in other eyes
I described it as I did
I tried to find the words to buy you
cut through to your pretty bones like kindness

You didn't love me with a vengeance
it was always coming true
am I lucky to be alive, my friend?
I've been expecting you

You probably don't remember me
the bad old days and so on
back when there was something wrong with love
little room, jumped-up ape
I kiss the floor and joke
"You're not the only child round here"
in seaweed paint I dance for you
round the ruins, round the view
the Helen & Menelaus Snack Bar
then you killed me off in theory
et in Arcadia ego
my feelings did so very much for you

The pain is so extraordinary
this pain in all its story tells me
pain's the best all purpose preservative
you were one of my better creations
everything's permitted I hereby swear
I cannot change this is how I see it
in these words not other words
nor at other times nor otherwise
nor otherwise nor otherwise

You didn't love me with a vengeance
it was always coming true
am I lucky to be alive, my friend?
I've been expecting you

KAREZZA

The atomic structure
of this caress
massive, silent and numb
as light as consciousness

The past is as silent
as the present is ancient
tirelessly evil
weary and patient

Colourful killer
brief cafe
real ice cream and power
baby mogul
mummy's back
to abhor and devour

Once upon a time
once upon a turbine
flying the world
dying of girls

BEAST BOX

The Beast Box
the Beast Box

Elvis Presley's body perfectly preserved

There's a lot of stories going around
I don't think it's right
are the neighbours really thinking
like you and me?
I woke up this morning
as clear as a bell on Judgment Day
I think it came open yesterday
they've opened the Beast Box, haven't they?
they've upset the Beast Box, haven't they?

Beast Box
Beast Box
Beast Box

In this dream I'm inside the Beast Box with my kid brother
and there are all these scenes of terrible suffering going on...

And I'm starting to feel really really ill...

In a dream I'm inside
I'm with my kid brother
there are scenes of awful suffering
we're avoiding looking at each other
then he's pointing to the handrail
it's long, of burnished chrome
and saying in that stupid voice of his
"Some of this would look really good
in the bathroom back home"

I woke up this morning
as clear as a bell on Judgment Day
they've upset the Beast Box
they've opened the Beast Box
haven't they?

Beast Box
Beast Box

They've opened the Beast Box, haven't they?

USELESS LOVE

Brittle shade
angel
son of manmade things
this love was written in waters that roar
this love that stops at nothing
that kills as it stings
this love that stops at nothing
that kills as it stings
it kills as it stings
this love you have no use for
this love you have no use for
that's written out in waters that roar
all the other characters wink
it's later than you think
it's always later than you think

Grainy
grey and rainy
wonders never cease
in the night of my human shape I saw
everybody's holding something back
they all want release
everybody's taking up the slack
they all want a piece
they all want a piece
of this love you have no use for
this love you have no use for
that's written out in waters that roar
all the other characters wink
it's later than you think
it's always later than you think

I wish to thank most warmly the musicians and composers, my partners past and present, for their respective roles in realising these *crimes passionnels* as songs: Barry Adamson, Robert Dickinson, Steve Diggle, John Doyle, Dave Formula, Martin Jackson, John Maher, Ben Mandelson, John McGeoch, Peter Shelley, Bernard Szajner; and, finally and most of all, Noko for Luxuria right now.

H.D.

DISCOGRAPHY OF RECORD ALBUMS

ARTIST & TITLE	UK LABEL	UK COMPACT DISC CATALOGUE NO.
BUZZCOCKS		
Time's Up	Release in preparation	
Spiral Scratch (EP)	Re-release in preparation	
MAGAZINE		
Real Life	Virgin	CDV 2100
Secondhand Daylight	Virgin	CDV 2121
The Correct Use of Soap	Virgin	CDV 2156
Play (live concert)	Virgin	CDV 2184
Magic, Murder And The Weather	Virgin	CDV 2200
After The Fact (compilation)	Virgin	*VM 1
Rays And Hail 1978-81 (compilation)	Virgin	COM CD5
BERNARD SZAJNER		
Brute Reason	Island	*ILPS 9735 (deleted)
HOWARD DEVOTO		
Jerky Versions Of The Dream	Virgin	CDV 2272
LUXURIA		
Unanswerable Lust	Beggars Banquet	BEGA 90 CD
Beast Box	Beggars Banquet	BEGA 106 CD

* vinyl album only